REPOSE

REPOSE

Amelia Zhou

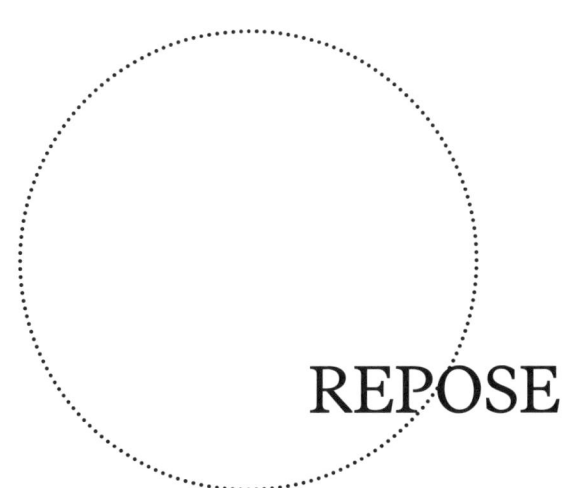

Wendy's Subway

THE LAST WORD WILL BE THE FOURTH DIMENSION.

Length: her speaking
Width: beyond thought
Depth: my speaking of her, of facts and feelings and of her beyond-thought.

I must be legible almost in the dark.

—Clarice Lispector

CONTENTS

DOES THE HOUSE PROTECT THE DREAMER

An idle kind of escape is how I have chosen to look —

I have chosen deceit, forthrightness, enough coy, around my finger coils the failed ringlet of hair —

Ask me why I am falling.   Breathless I complete the end then action of desire.   I am here to play exchange until I can deceive no longer.   Until my empty pose slips into best fit and so on to the next survival exercise —

In my executions I exceed me.   All stratum of debt exceeds me. Miniature problems, minor feelings, invoiced for publics.   Bills made on a machine line, designed not to reject or fray.   I am duplicate upon duplicate, accepting learning to accept nothing from the exchange —

That radical passage.   Everything coming from nothing.   A loss, facades an unconscious, upside down ends the archway, so crystalline my belief gravity is.   Once was.   Holding up the weight as if I.   As if I were someone who owned all I could carry of myself —

To bloom out the ragged bud, I strayed from one education to evanescent other and called it accumulation.   Seasons.   One after another, my plain mistakes became the fact I am most real and living.   After living, the pressing matter of the day: that of duration under same duress —

I am in:

A common secret.

The occupation requires me to cover myself with my body for several work years as necessary.

Early in the years, I learn to regard my body and what happens to it as something that happens to someone else.

In return, I am granted a second body. She is applied to the outside of my first body: in medical terms, a remedy. She is expected to heal all diseases, as a draught and salve.

When applied, she cures and cures.

Results yield a feeling of nothing for a long duration of time. Nothing can be a pleasant feeling, but usually not for a long duration of time.

A second body is therefore defined by not having a pleasant feeling for a long duration of time. Symptoms of being overrun and seized by intruders. One by one till no more room in the sanctuary. Intruders pre-bend doors to take possession. Nothing becomes impersonal to me because everything is rightfully owned by those who step into my occupancy.

In my occupation as real estate agent, I know all about criteria for occupancy.

My home is a house of multiple occupancy because no owner applies: My history my voice my clef my privacy my tears. Her whisper her yes her lies her recitation no privacy no tears. Their honor their heads their speech

My address?

Complaint: mouth is far away from voice
Occupants: ears are far away from complaint

And tears naturally pool.   Water her vision extract moisture from stone absorbs in walls of the house.   Talking at occupants complaints of her body collect in foundations then pools in walls of the house.

The entire touch is wet.
The entire touch dries with sum of sweat, saliva,

Outcome?

absence painted water   stains
surface of stain   kept
well protected by secret

oldfashionedhardwhitesoap.

So. Defaced sequence goes:

a) I facelift her new head
b) Apply wide range of concealers until someone else is left
c) Now pick the dusty pink shadow and highlight
d) Angle a few dots against the tear duct, to make sure eyes are moist, regularly
e) Reinforce by using eye drops, regularly

Left untreated, leaks cause rotting and rest of the house to become damp.

Her, watched = price of admission.

When house opens for inspection and she is real estate agent of the house:

a) Be careful, do not open walls or other imperishable exteriors
b) Remember, point to every glittered inch and carpets

Her mouth now wandering away. Her mouth enters into model kitchen.

"Look!"

She says.

The preparation required to build, vanish, and sell, including the preparation of herself, herself intruded by others becoming intruders becoming occupants becoming market determinants of whole valuation project predetermined.

Her qualifications include assisting buyers and sellers in purchasing and selling property for the right price under the best terms, valuing the right price, maximizing value, market analysis, excellent trustworthiness in action.

"Plus, far-reaching views, complete seclusion, and the grounds are magnificent," she said.

Up the steps, the real estate agent practices her mouth better and better with public speaking skills. A frock coat, starched with new folds, ordinates lifelong walks and talks. A career progressing ruins into diamonds

because this time, she's someone else. Her mouth on behalf says,

"Excellence!" "Intermediary!"

To lose own language or speak estimation. Substitute for substitute, she and I organize ourselves in twos. Inside

play the steady game of division

which exists only for work and not to live:

Fantasy is not appropriate when exchanging mouth with lost wages. Fantasy is only appropriate when occupants mark mouth for improvement.

Nevertheless

, In order to live

she is inside the house, fantasizing outside of trustworthy decision making. There are ifs for herself and herself alone. If disappear into foundations. In foundations of the house, secret wet ruins. Secret wet ruins weep blood. Foundations weep blood. If weeping were a flood,

Can she weep her lost mouth back from ruins?

Do all lost things live in ruins?

If here she is

. . . swimming . . . swimming . . .
sinking

the water —

Like fantasy is never enough.

Mouth is never enough.

Excavation is a natural state.

The work of digging, and more exacting, the work of the spade.

That familiar scene for real estate agents:

windowsoverinfinity
edgepool
overlooking

So you are right on top of everything.

And so much blood in the foundations

. . . *catch it&breathe out* . . .
an opposite

alive —

I wade into the house which, although blighted by decay, is very much a nice house.

I find her in the model kitchen, eating damp leftovers.

In every house we ever lived, if ruins weren't diamonds.

If occupants have no part in it all.

In order of failed, renovated, wet.

To fill = we'll gut.

Used for almost three hundred years under single ownership, the house is put up for auction with no reserve.

"We're excited for what the future holds for our finest home.

"We're hopeful the new owners will accrue," the former occupants said.

, having been immaculately maintained ever since —

, its restored interior equally as timeless —

"We'll miss the sun come through these big windows!"

When asked to describe her intent on selling the house, the real estate agent said, "I've learned to know the average occupant, what it is they want, and they all want the most exclusive price for a spare house in hideaway country.

"I knew I had to follow own instructions. I knew I had to sell the house for lost wages. There are renovation plans all the time,"

and if they aren't done yet

, on a house once listed for millions —

, forever incompletes our bid —

"We'll watch the sun come through these big windows!"

With

out disappearing.   Sough

the after.   Picture now   the after

math of blood stained;   impossible falls

inside the house.

Before us, two doors, treasury to our treachery.

But grandeur and desolation in which

I—

Enter I:

Shut the door:

Let her in

:

A WHOLE BODY
IS COMPLETE
THEREFORE USABLE

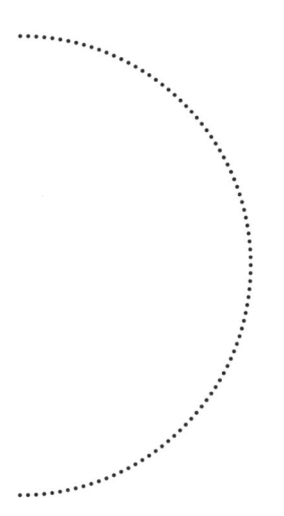

and that starting so
poorly, I can live

—Alice Notley

I am in a room that is open late and helps me stay sane.

What resembles a bedroom except the sign says surgery and beneath the sign, on the reception desk, there are dozens of shrink-wrapped garments awaiting their new owners.

A dream does not deceive, this is a doctor's waiting room.

So, I wait for my name to be called — the name I've been given to put on myself.

Imagine perhaps:

A muffled yet imperious voice calls out from the periphery of the room.

A beat of silence, before it demands again, then again.

When spoken over the shoulder like that, the name is received like an unwelcome question.

Listen.

To get myself screwed right I must locate the correct folder and quarter-inch hex key; file an interim report reviewing my face, authority, and lack of, et cetera; then revive the other inside my bedside drawer, for my hibernation resides there, abandon of I.

I know I can make anything possible by pressing enter.

Entry leads to another file that spells "return."

From the plastic green chair I get up to go drink from the water cooler, keep drinking in a rather uncritical kind of way, watching fellows, doctors, and standard-set officers saunter the carpeted hallways outside.

A face (whose?) — scowling — reflects off the water cooler.

Now I am a passenger, I can't stop searching for myself.

En route to the reception desk, in the deadtime of the queue, I think about my garment options. I decide to wear my best, most expensive coat, reserved for special occasions such as birthdays, driving lessons, board meetings, weekly grocery trips, and appointments. The would-be story weaves into daily dress. The goal of the story is so one is primed for life's profession — that's readiness.

Hope: my haute couture outfit will impress, land me that story I'm counting on, been working on for months.

It is now the sixteenth day after my scheduled appointment.

My last hope: being able to rise to the occasion.

`Thank you so much for waiting.`

`You've done your job.`

`It's so nice of you to be so`
`organized ready to go.`

Doctor finally turns around, pushes glasses up nose, smiling, seems happy to see me.

I, on the other hand, put on a smile not quite as dazzling as it could be.

After all, I am going to undergo a procedure I am not sure will go well, not knowing the procedure, whatever doctor is trying to do.

Through the hallway, into doctor's office. Utilitarian mirror, wash basin, plastic dressing table, walls identical to the ceiling — wallpapered with cherubs on blue.

Notice the doctor wearing a coat similar to mine, though do not read this in comparison to my own aspirations
or career.

Me? Do I have
any plans?

Go to doctor to remind myself what my next
steps should be. Eight days ago, I visited doctor to listen to the same story for the first time. I know nothing and do not ask. I knew this lesson, I already learned.

A girl learns
before long,

another lesson
will knock —

At the mantel, the doctor stands, expressionless.

```
Excuse me, you seem familiar.
Have you been to this clinic
before?
```

To sew garments alone and graft another coat upon my person.

So doctor examines the plaster.

So doctor will remove with tweezers.

Doctor holds tweezers like one would a lollipop or chocolate ice cream cone.

Don't lick, don't touch, a
metallic sharp thing like
that is not meant to be
enjoyed much less eaten.

I advise you look away.

Turn away,
face emptying
through the
window.

Better yet, close your eyes.

See: nothing to
be seen.

Relax! Treat my dressing
table like your sofa.

I seize its
plastic covers.

Outside, enter the desolate flattery of my sabotage-self hopelessly as ever.

Inside, the color shifts red.

Blush the same color as behavior.

Not the kind of fire that burns.

`How does it taste?`

`How does it feel in your mouth?`

So much for sustenance.

I know all the answers to typical questions doctor asks.

I open my eyes and do not want to speak again.

Awake.

To dreamt forgotten.

Memory!
Memory!   Disappears the longer I sleep.

First, unlock bedside drawer. Inside drawer, manila folder. Get out folder. Search through its papers. Doctor has another question for you. So take off your coat. Sit down. Say nothing, you tell yourself, or lose your name.

> When did you begin. What happens when you. You need to be willing to talk. So, tell me about your histories. Tell me about your illicit histories. For instance, how old were you when you were first diagnosed. Where did you go from there. It doesn't seem possible that you.
>
> What else.
>
> Such as.

It is possible without feeling any effects.

Doctor takes manila folder, red pencil, information.

```
What I want is to have your
story and its details right.

It's the only way I can
understand.
```

Lesson VIII

Familiarize yourself with the art of taking.

I'm a doctor, there's nothing wrong with you, do what I tell you and I'll determine there's nothing wrong with you, so get well soon, I hope you feel better soon, I want you to be well as I'm thinking of you, praying for your speedy recovery, I'll be back, I'm going to be back, I'll see you soon whenever you're free, could be in a month, maybe two, you must be better then, certain I promise.

Q. But doctor, what does it say about me that I have to repeat what I have to say every time?

A. Please take care of yourself.

By eating the right food for your body.

Lesson IX

To be happy I must have a room of my own and take care of myself by eating the right food for my body.

To be stable, unimpeachable, free of qualification problems and difficulties.

To receive the line between proper care and improper cure, irrespective.

Granted,

With the tacit approval of someone.

Whose goal is to become.

Fact is, I'm very interested in diagnosis.

I know you would understand,

As a white collar.

So, doctor,

Another question,

What is the diagnosis of doubt?

Q. Please describe a time in your life when you were successful, proud, free from rupture, everything as per, decimal place.

A. Read, or better yet, scream what's written on the paper scraps that have fallen out of your folder, in no particular order:

I am wearing a small and lovely cut on my finger and a white asymmetrical dress beneath my coat that both cost more than the pay I live in.

As a young girl, I thoroughly believed there was no method of being better than a cloth in tatters.

By age twelve, the poverty of my departure (spiritual and economic) had been solidified.

Admitting that I have problems is a mode of optimism, because every problem has a solution.

Now it is the seventeenth day after my scheduled appointment, and I am on a different page of the floor plan.

There I began with your final word.

This place is mine and mine alone.

Years later, I walked out early from a lecture at school wearing your name on my hand.

Can I please blame my actions on the lacking infrastructure?

Yes, I never stopped, not even at the emergency exit of the world.

With my running sneakers on, I thought I could easily evade capture, but would that be a guarantee of freedom?

En route, I thought of my excreted scraps, naked and patient on the waiting room floor, giving birth to their own secret poem.

Listen, now, again.

I write with the speed I write without waiting for myself any longer.

But I cannot answer back besides give and take accountancy: tallying up twenty green pennies, my faithful hex key, plus five metro tickets in my pockets,

How to pay or not the ransom of compliance that you demand between us,

Someone born on this interchange of freeway is destined to wander crosswinds and crossings, left ahead, permanent signs.

Most fail to flourish when care is taken to alleviate exclusively like honey.

I don't know the best outfit to pick when confronted by a dozen or so choices.

I don't know how far I can continue to run with my vital organs leaking out of my coat pockets.

An appointment is overdue to remove myself from you.

Yes, I've paid upfront at the reception desk.

Behind, a trail of my outskirts and suffixes.

Describe: the cost of four-by-four space.

Lesson X

Outside, darkness is falling and visibility is close to zero, so please, do not get extinguished.

Do not get tempted to follow permanent signs that lead to plush-carpeted hallways, wellbeing clinics, or worse.

When you arrive at the place inscribed in the secret poem, keep running (for this place is not your destination), but look briefly toward where you had been.

You face a questionable open, as where you begin is a view of a house receding; it recedes now to somewhere else, no longer there, no longer found.

But night.

Night!

Who keeps knocking on the distant door?

Say dream.

Who are you to answer?

NOW
THE TERROR
PRESENT IN THE
ANXIETY OF TOTAL SKY

Someone's screaming?[I]

No?

You didn't hear anything?

No?

Put your ear to the ground.

Why?

Why else, this shatter in the floor?[II]

I Do you remember how beautiful our past was?

II I do not know what you mean.

Dreamphase: once upon a time eight years later around three in the morning sixteen years ago in spring birthmarked the afternoon turned evening when sun on this day rose upon a woman's delayed return to the land of her childhood inside the time a girl first leaves her home know this greeting cannot spring back it cannot be repeated once three in the dark leans into fugitive cold of February night after night approaches the sea of winter approaching years arc minutes once nested and vague

Dreamcontents in order of frequency:

1. Loved ones
2. Work
3. Erotic
4. Surgery
5. Obsession preoccupation lasting doubt
6. Fairy tale
7. Motor charge e.g. running away failing flying not dead maybe dying
8. Protest

I travel somewhere to swim with my lovers let's make the water our secret domain though where I lie invited by waves lies a greater temptation for inventory the temptation curls towards a repletion I do not recognize it does not belong to me so I must tempt operator there are many like you arresting then enclosing to take the wrapped coastline out of their eyes

....but nothing can cure the incurable and therapy a terminal reminder of fact for instance once I presented an architectural paper to an audience so non-receptive to my so-called ideas that for years after on occasions when I visited the national gallery I would see baroque portraits laughing as if they were characters in a political caricature though the subject of said caricature was not one you could say induced much laughter hence I remained resolute for the whole of the very expensive session though acting outside

....................................so foolish was this experience I became a girl of naive collection almost without belief someone you would give to an operator she scarcely knew because she is handsome and they are equally handsome and it is submission to affection she desires as she believes sovereignty can be found in such lovely besides loveless flight

..................................operator of course is inebriated jealous influential guilty of grandiose acts intensive labors to destroy her affections they accuse her of making them an extremely sane and competent mad-doctor mad and so bestows the reciprocal making of her own madness by way of teaching english behavior as to complete her as to isolate her from the world mundane small acts like she drops her gloves you pick them up she drops her gloves you pick them up and you look happy she looks bored and she is bored so you are pleased

.........................separation from operator imparts a new belief to shed all parts of herself to reconstitute a reality of herself true by matter of delusion fixation error her erroneous desire for phantoms who circle circle back around themselves who profess revolution to no resolution always a girl learns harder and alone

....slowly over
an unknown period of time all the fictions of the same beautiful
landscape that falsified unflourished her understanding begin
to depose for this conjuncture wishes for the precise sort of
rupture that unravels completely so completely I shall hope what's
fated yours is long as an architecture befallen into tragedy I
now revenge mine

.....................beneath the proscenium under maximum stage lights everything came back to myself my full perils and privations as if I was looking for myself as if everyone was looking for me at me staring staring seeing at me and finding not a semblance I surge between two shores from apparent course of normal sun to some other parallel inside some other dream where another dreams of faint refuge reasons for my own unreason because where I reside

rifts from nowhere

their very old crumbling dream

....& I walk these coastlines

bone&body..
....
....
....
....
..................blood&body..
....
....
....
....
....
....drop

bloody
&
breath

....
....
....
....
....asking
howheavydoyoumakeyourhead...
....
....
....
....
....
....

when you watch the world

from this angle

HOW FAR
HER HAIR BLOWS
BACK IN THE HARD
HEADWIND
OF FALL

the rest of the time I lived in a lyric
—what else?—like all lunatics.

—Pier Paolo Pasolini

The longer she held onto an idea of being tied to place, the more she believed in emergent stagnancy, a being held in solidification proceeding removal from heat (how many minutes ago?)

She desired to be subject in drama rather than liquid witness, to withdraw herself from certain expected questions and certain expected answers, though realizing this desire long after the fact.

For memory is a tense still being written, so what she knew in the moment was net with sediment passing through, meeting scraps of confusion, refusal, and odd direction, same-change then chance.

She entertained a counterintuitive travel, valentining freefall as elimination of anything resembling symmetry or wholeness, as she believed there were more discovered ways to verify a path — to let weight bear onto different, yes other, planes.

In this preset, there was no requirement for destination, it became question of measuring vitality before order, then how far that may go — how far her hair blows back in the hard headwind of fall.

I want to live in everything that happens beyond the barrier of the picture frame.

Where the whole does not perish but a part will survive, whose persistence is discontinuous.

I look for cut-off elements, her shape and her hand, that shape described by her absence.

Sometimes, that absence is you.
Sometimes, that's part of the figure.

An urgent choreography tries to catch up all the time.

The inside of undoing that painting.

There I hold myself in valleys between each finger.

There I billow — dissolute — what instance is form.

1. (At which point does her world unfold)
2. (At which point does she identify an "is" is happening)
3. (At which point does one position fall to another)

Multiplication of plot — meadow — country. Where hard fact meets a toss in the break begin pleats of an embrace.

I put breath into opacity and see my edges screen into porous limitation, dreamed fabric of membrane.

A seed puts vision on the line and sews information in the field of play.

Sediment and its steps.

How biology distinguishes its web.

That I am whole cell interpenetrated with environment: breath and its offering.

My ribcage.

Deep sponge.

To the left: a radiation.

To turn my palm and absorb sun as epidermal sensation.

And I try to live in the tensile before movement becomes evaporation.

To bend, crease, wrinkle; sense of yield to pressure; sedimentary strata surging from permanent deformation; doubling upon oneself; I move my body closer to you; undo finality of form.

I think relationally of a fold as a hug between us, tied together in this thing we're in.

Knot, or is it backbone: standing particles, hazel beam, the vital categories of matter — all simultaneous not sequential events.

What I desire (duration inside this compression)

Seepage of our lineages, morphogenesis from feather to bud. She who sinks, dress spreading out in flower, her arms reach to stretch around your space.

Of surface wave tracking undulation of your spine —

Of pressing gently in fold, rather than stopping energy at the border —

Of incipiency buoyed by what is extending toward you —

Thresholds come naturally and can lead anywhere

(How I feel of an epidermal one[I]

(How much the boundary bled[II]

....

I curtain of heat

II returning into dissolving generator

FORMS OF A CAREER (FUNDAMENTAL LIFE)

Limbs

(Disciplined silk dress)

Hair

(Tall wavy back, extending above stage)

Head

(Say you're very good at the mirror, painful pain in your eyes)

Skin

(Fabrication of you then the rest of you)

Muscles

(Peripheral pain in hands, pain in legs, pain in hips, meaning long-term sequence)

Knees

(And so on, was it always memory, of bone to practice next)

(Who moves closer to the distance you are carrying, circumstance into that distance

(When behind the curtain — heart was closing — was opening waves —

The female dancer appears on stage without apparent history — without sweat, without tears, without gravity, without weight. She is reliant on the stage alone as the sheer basis of her existence.

A momentary life which exists as long as her promenade on one foot for two minutes and forty-six seconds.

She has mastered the art of being on the receiving end of a look.

From where I sit in the second circle balcony, row A, seat number seventeen.

Here are a few plots of a turn: promenade, pirouette, grand jeté en tournant, fouetté, posé, changement, waltz.

All require phenomenal control to execute without faltering, falling, an inch of misstep.

Success also depends on the supposed natural rotational potential of the hips.

One particular evening, a woman, clearly in mental anguish, puts her hands over her eyes, palms facing out to the audience, fingers splayed (three seconds). Suddenly finds herself on stage without knowing why, something like water behind her. Accompanist on the piano. Silver silk bias cut dress. White plimsolls, bottoms unmarked. You won't believe me, but I have no memory of what happened before. She starts to dance again, as a lucky escape.

Turning over and over for the next countless hour.

The character of a story, like the dancer on stage, inhabits a present-continuous gesture for the duration of their reception by the audience.

I look up the etymology of *gesture*:

"manner of carrying the body"
"bearing, behavior, mode of action, carriage, posture"
"action taken to express feeling"
"a movement of the body or part of it"

She walks out of view with her arms held still by her side taking the long route of the whole perimeter of stage (thirty-five seconds).

It is precisely the simplicity of the walk — its dictated slow poise, the ordinary steps — that commands attention. Her presence transforms into passage (thirty-five seconds).

And thus closes the first act.

One freedom of the dancer is that they often appear conspicuous yet recede into what seems to be an unknown course of events in simultaneous time. Now and now and now: the dancer bends space-time and inhabits it through innumerable forms. A present that sustains its own origins is the dancer's myth. If dance exhibits anything it is its innate medial character: between the spectrum of movement and arrest, the tremble and the bravura turn *en pointe*, a dancer's gestures make visible a continual metamorphosis of a whole, of which those gestures are part.

Now unfold the layers of the performance as to become palimpsest of a life.

Buoyed by the logics of inscrutability, I step into the day: its frame, its costume, its veiled universal grammar.

Here I am compelled to tell the unremarkable story of a girl who tries to reconcile the external image of her existence — the way she is perceived, understood, and fictioned, by others, across all manner of verbs — with her desire to get closer to her image of herself, to see her own eyes toward herself.

The story starts by erasure into someone else's dream. Then scenes change so quickly from one cut to another I can never remember; that's how disappearance goes.

(Only a feelingbelief
it keeps repeating —

The Saint Laurent dream! Called this girl from nowhere and she's also an illusion.

Is how she knows herself a sentence of command?

Is she for or against or within herself?

Dancer and choreographer Carol Brown on improvisational strategies to locate the other within: “To fix in space-time and then to undo by decodings, spasms, wrenchings, blurrings, and breakages.”

)

“With reckless impetuous gestures—break line—break gender—break sound—break center.”

So doubt begins to be introduced to the status of the image.

And where did she end up?

Daily, I step into the day with nothing but a style to make my image my own. Garments of choice include sentimentalism, melodrama, confession, ornamentation, assemblage. Like many, reluctance and vehemence to all things work. Escape is my relentless obsession. And dreams, a form of compensation. Where I take my leave forever.

In the Saint Laurent S/S 2022 show, it was impossible to miss the waterfall from which each model emerged, miraculously dry and dressed in deviations of evening jackets and silk-skin jumpsuits. And the sly clutch bag slipped into the waistband, something the designer had seen Picasso do with a theatre program in a paparazzi shot back in the day.

How do I perform or not perform?

Begin by orienting east, then pan up and sideways into the place of the girl who has already gone away. To where, I don't know. It is worth trying to counterfeit yourself to find yourself. Steal the Saint Laurent silk-skin jumpsuit. For this instant of the story, wear it as an extravagant masquerade. If this sounds absurd, it's because I have displaced the reality of reality. But the jumpsuit could be a method to strike an artful figure out of the frame. To fled, missing, or lost? Time upon time, she becomes someone seen too much or not at all.

The dancer was remarkable in her ability to rotate lightly, the most serene of expressions on her face.

When the curtains closed, and the demands for an encore began, she responded with a new volley of pirouettes, no sign of fatigue (thirty-two rotations).

The execution of her balletic technique was incomparable in all respects, almost ideal.

The longer one practices certain techniques in rehearsal, the smoother the performance for which they are required can proceed. The body has a remarkable propensity for consolidating complicated movements in muscle memory through repetition. One's memory of how to execute the sequence is never far away.

For example, I know the thirty-two fouettés were achieved almost perfectly in the performance, because it felt entirely unexceptional.

I had complete control.

In John Cassavetes's film *Opening Night*, we follow the tribulations of stage actress Myrtle Gordon as she prepares for her starring role in the soon-to-premiere play, *The Second Woman*. Throughout the film, those around her offer unsolicited assurances:

> *Everyone loves you.*
> *You're a woman.*
> *You're so good at being a woman you're not a woman you're a professional.*
> *You're a super high-priced professional.*

Who is Myrtle?

a) A woman with no ties: guiltless, loveless, defiant, no responsibility to anyone but herself, which leaves her vulnerable.
b) A woman who confuses her dreams and fantasies with reality for so long that she must put an end to these fantasies, but this leaves her going on stage feeling nothing no awareness of who I am what I am wanting herself back.

On the opening night of *The Second Woman*, Myrtle decides to abandon the playscript to portray her character as she wants. She changes her lines. She improvises an arch-identity striptease. Breaks character, returns to her. Transgresses the written-in boundaries of her character's fate. Regains herself by taking the character's fate as hers and hers alone to fiction into reality through the present-continuous process of its live unfolding. I can make the character appear or disappear at will, her actions seem to say. The so-called super high-priced professional takes over in a moment of psychic exchange to seek control over an image of herself she may well never get. *I am not me! There's someone posing here as us!* Her performance is received by the audience with rapturous applause.

Is it possible to be noticed by others and free? I think of this line by Fanny Howe when I step out of the cinema, imagining Myrtle still there on stage acting up more arch-possibility, a possibility that exceeds the closing titles of the film and runs off into the opening sequence of another, yet to be made.

○

A large part of my self-education was learning that when I enter a space, the scene had already been set.

It requires hard work not to see:

a) The girl is shading her eyes from the viewer
b) The girl is silent and lounging
c) The girl's face is inscrutable
d) The girl is wearing beautiful silks
e) And ceramics alongside which she sits

Because on every occasion, she is careful not to disturb the viewer's eye. Because in her retreat, she knows the most effective strategy is to make up a fantasy that pleases.

The occasion repeats and turns into a sequence. The sequence is a girl who chases around and around for her own image. Could she compose an image with no edges, her secret grammar extending to touch everything except its frame. But where she is permitted to go. Idealism and dainty escapism cannot forever maintain themselves. She walks the route of the indefinite perimeter until someone asks where she has been.

The girl who comes from nowhere and she's also an illusion.
The girl who clings to the same dress and gives her daily sunning, generation after generation.
The girl mired in the image of the other.

Is more than anyone could ever see.

So I write through fragmentation and variance. I consider the ways in which fragments of myself hold together, fragments selecting fragments, fragments turning whole from instructions. Pan over. The image is more than anyone could ever see. Pan over. From mouth to mouth, parts of her speech open her tongue was it her tongue. Zoom in. Remember, here lies the chronic subplot beneath the worded.

Zoom out.

In the blurred light, veil over her face, she seemed to gesture toward the pose held in her imagination.

Freeze.

○

When I step onto the stage, there is a notable absence of nerves. My face is devoid of readable expression. I have an impossible talent for discretion. You read this as a sign of self-control. I appear unaffected by the common commotion going on around me for the rest of the scene. Remember, the mask-like characteristics of my face are so perfectly blank to become her. *Because once you're convincing in a part*, says Myrtle Gordon, *the audience accepts you as that*.

To be convincing requires effort to maintain over the years, so I try to submerge myself, totalize into her form.

Her form is impossible because one is always more than anyone could ever see.

But I am convinced I should get closer, or to the ends, of the impossibilities of knowing myself.

Because every girl needs her own style through which the body can be reinvented, redefined, made variant like the sky or weather. And the sun which shines through the pane this morning like that adds a point of difference. There is one side of the glass then I travel through to the other. Reassess the image. Reflect on the reincarnation. This morning, like every morning, there is the effort of fulfilling definition. Potential is a girl who has her eyes toward herself, who sees her possibilities unfolding freely to herself, even as all the time, she grows more elusive. So she can flee from the inheritance of herself. So she can insist on the realness of that figure.

And I know that figure is real because I kept the notebooks in which I wrote these words to know that I have lived.

Through dreams of reversibility, plots of instantaneous resistance, deviant locomotion at a distance, and her own voluntary deceits, a girl can live a little more like herself. The category through which she is seen is also a category of metamorphosis. The category in which I made my introduction, ceaselessly. There she goes, into the next turn.

I witness the performance unfold in front of my eyes from where I sit, motionless and silent, apart from the parts of myself swept into its production.

The choreographic death pang of Giselle, who collapsed before a sound left her mouth.

> *That is the strain I loved — the waltz I danced to —*
> *the fatal Wili waltz — once more I tread its steps . . .*
>
> *Rob me not of this last poor pleasure . . . ah! my steps*
> *falter — my limbs grow faint — I choke — I*

If all one has is one's furious dignity —

What does one make of oneself in the face of one who —

I HAVE ONLY ONE OCCUPATION LEFT: TO REMAKE MYSELF

before I am lost,
hell must open like a red rose
for the dead to pass.

—H.D.

columns & worn; entrance & white; worth & anothertime; sometimes & same; punctuated & her traces; I & her traces; partitioned & immobile; to abandon & absolve dimming; speeches cast & all white material; speak all this & cast the material; obvious dimming & brief pause in; again, my pause & barely, either; wishing metamorphosis & viciously, I pray; prayer is necessary & to justify present; neither mine & made, her scribe; already

it's said & only to say;
endurance resold &
salve, my speech; sting
yet sting & bared, at
sight; citing lost particle
& purposed a full;
flung inside organ
& memory on chord;
necessary but &
knowledged, a rank;
many mornings pretend
& bandit resemblance;
brilliant sun mornings
& civilization, song;
stops into requisition &
I & doubt; propel
refractions of & out
to a same; deeply those
laps & wind its first
sound; implant my
superseding & name

my accord; enough
barely quite & still
to full stop;
immobilizing nearer
& the whole,
directs; ornamentation
awed & or motion
veined; arterial defense
& translucence type
skin; mutates pastpast &
errs transparent mark;
souvenirs in exhalation
& uh utters where;
down goes down &
I cannot accept;
deceptive refuge
& motion in vain;
entrance is made &
stagnant an air;
againagain & given
its taketh

I've been working here for years but this place probably isn't real. Something in me is being removed. Don't know what. But whatever it is it is. What I say has been repeated before and what I really want to say I've dreamed night after night already. When I wake I place one foot in front of the other. Slowly. Very, very slowly. Look at my body in bed. Is it more comfortable to be a dreamer or remain asleep? Leave my name and number. Dream ends when I turn the key to the door.

I'm dressed in a shot-silk gown sitting cross-legged in the office waiting for superior's offer. Say I've been looking forward to this moment. Say alternative phrases and other lies. Superior hands over a nondescript binder. Page one / part a) / you are not an individual. Eyes skim page four / section three / you consent to being listed and taken as proprietor of our company's new subsidiary. *I hope you can accept my offer,* superior says. Unique opportunity to make this baby yours, create a lasting inheritance beyond generation, because that's what we need / infusion of fresh blood to maximize our family's chance of survival. Fact. *Raising a baby isn't a complicated job.* Fact. *You're our best dreamer to make these fortunes flesh.*

Describe the ingredients of your new venture: on ground floor, baby is born. Because legacy is the primary aim of a family, baby must be fed. So treat baby like a domestic animal. Maybe a dog. Most people like dogs. Second, if you don't feed a dog that must be kept stronger and growing what it really, really wants, dog won't tolerate the desperation. Turns into brute. So search for key nutrients. A means to survive. To prevent excess blood loss. But satiation comes at a cost. Consider parts of yourself expendable, or easily replaced. For example, pretense of money / ornamental attitude / material goods bought with pretense of money / an oxygen of confidence confidence confidence. In other words, baby, I'll do anything for you. Because we're family. Because we're in the business of taking care of each other. *Yes, baby. I'll paint your skyscraper in perfume-red.*

Baby. Rewinds through rotten beginning. And I count on my fingers many. Cartilage mineralizes to bone then deterioration bequeaths a newborn. Efforts a shallow breath to cope with outside world. For decades baby has lived and therefore its last breath returns sharper / perpetually / as it ascends the floors intent on weightless / go back to first. Wheezes. Ages. How long do I have to keep reading the contract. A watch doesn't know but gaze into a crystal ball it'll give twenty bucks gut feel of how tall skyscraper will be, medium to long term. Jump cut to day zero I'm printing multiple copies bringing documents to the meeting. The safest course is to execute with formality. My last act as a kind and willing host. If the crystal ball is right, I'm on slow track to survive / and look / always there's a wild gulf just thriving. By end of contract, whiplashed in its *mise-en-scène*.

Hold on.

Intermission.

Let my standard lines play a role here.

It's a great compulsion of mine to be in this position. I went to school. I went to college. Was taught how to wash my hands deliberately and very well. I washed my hands I went to work then sat at the ivory tablecloth sugaring baby's wine deliberately and very well. And after work. End of day / end of week / end of patience / repeat simple patterns such as ticking formidable forms / fix dead language of reports / stage management of not working at work / grand finale of flying into a meeting to discuss some frivolous little fire when I'd rather preside the house burning but that's defiance against the rules. By the time I land I'm a madwoman in the desert with a target pinned to your mirage. I've seen all manner of your treacherous lies before. Baby pays and I have paid my exit taxes. But damn you for the latter. The way out only happens in the secrecy of my dream.

Is this what timeless means to you? Baby chews on my teats, leaving inkjet shadow around my nipples. Tiny hands slide down my waist. Every twenty-five take a screen break in the office restroom mirror to touch up lips with a surrogate lipstick. They say don't bite the hand that feeds you, but I'm a fool like a dog and a dog will always bite another fool like me. Baby's hopeless disobedience is an appetite which exists to return again. And yes, so will mine, demand me back from the restroom mirror, I too can bite and bite / feed a brute pieces of its own foolish mouth. Until wheezes. Ages. What follows / go back to the first of no epoch. Because I'm obedient, I'm urgent, I'm a professional, I write with your mouth I write with all insatiable mouths, feed you documents from which you're written, print your spit put it back on the shelf. Later in the meeting I say, *baby, of course, it goes without saying*. All these complicated words are going to run out of print by the time I'm done — I wake up made-up and ready.

Change focal point /

Scene /

Method. Letter by letter I demolish. It's my technique. My absolute priority. I make priceless impressions with my monomaniacal parenting skills meanwhile my mouth is running out becoming just an idea. The idea being I predict one day all you know will betray you. It's a matter of what's next on the course. Baby, don't you worry the final contract is the perfect size of your fill-me-up stomach. Look at me how I look while I'm carrying you, dagger of the narrative, reaping my womb of mercurial temper until you devour the cashless black hole. Inside me can't disappear any longer. Inside me open windows / doors / walls / office restroom mirrors and let desecration spread. Ascend to ivory headquarters which is only ivory no other characteristics. This is where baby's signature goes. Do you know when this dream ends? Please. I was here before my whole body was proof. I spoiled and spoiled by entry. I spoil and spoil into baby's wine at the dinner table.

Now listen.

Mummy mummy mummy. Falling from baby's eyes into its cup a sticky liquid — is it ink or blood? In my dream there's a night sky out the top floor and it's almost daybreak, almost too late to write off baby down the elevator into expiration, because it wants to sit idly cry its tears sip its regurgitated wine waiting for others to dry out first. But baby you got me wrong, I was never the type of patient woman who liked to whittle away lounging around in a chair. Still,

I'll wait as you descend slowly to dregs, wake up open my eyes wide watch you behave like a worn brute on a leash, just as you always loved to beg I act on behalf for you, as if yes is the answer yet no is my answer because it is I who choose in between. I choose I choose. I look into the crystal ball. My hands are poised / prepared to do. I'm doing / have done your bidding. I never took a vacation from you. Who owns a face, who owns its words, I cannot say yes for yet another second of my time. Close my hands walk into empty cup stop baby's tongue of complicated words pull my name from inside baby's body. And if the crystal ball has any part in it, the end plays out with nothing left just a scream of dried cries and I standing by in the tide of your wake. *Yes I'm dead! I'm dead!* Baby's tears echo on and on in insolent song. Why does it take so long for echoes to stop? I couldn't tell you. I'm so bored of your form.

Mummy mummy mummy

The song of indifferent intervals
The song of lies and lies on the other side
Is that the sound of mummy being taken away

When the song of baby is gone?

Oops. The dagger I throw is blunt and concise. Catch me if you can, red-handed if you can, if you know when to look in the restroom mirror. Tonight, like every night, when dagger lands in the basement and baby languishes into backlog, full of capsized motion the same beliefs, just as I've always known that below the lit horizon, before the negative view, in the skyscraper where I work, the documents I've printed conclude to fumes on your shelves. Please blow out the fire quickly. Please the fire no longer raged. All the evidence you left behind is the last sign of who you were. Now here I am blazed in smoke searching for my metaphorical exit. From path to path, a chance to desert or sky? Because I'm a woman with ambition, I fly with stage prop wings pinned on my back, paper blue wings, so big they strangle the sky. I go to school / I go to work / I get lost in the mirage / crossing never escaping the edge, counting down the seasons until ivory tablecloth wipes up baby's tears. When the horizon finally clears, I'm far away with my gaze saturated with oceans great and thin. Perhaps what I see announces the proper end of the world, or maybe the top, depending on how this sky is composed. What were you doing there, getting born and born like nothing happened? In every dream, I miss hearing the tides with their faint faint sighing at night. *Three times fainter, three times fainter, three times fainter,* the ashes sigh, so long the ashes dispersed into sea.

(WHILE MY HOUSE CONTINUES TO ROTATE ON EARTH

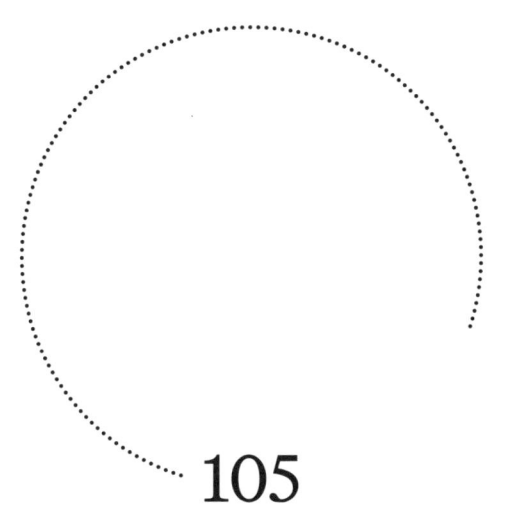

Like everywhere else, a policy of destruction is being followed.

Because all your life, you wanted your career to get to yes.

You close the deal, then people lived with that deal.

Cooperation makes a big secret out of this quest.

All that distinguishes is
a reminder there is
something still from the
secret

,   accreting

We sleep through
dereliction, sinister and
silent,

hunting

for our angels:

NOTES

This book completes as an album. A list of sources and quotes, directly referenced or alluded to in the book, are attributed below to the best of my memory.

p. 5: Lispector, Clarice. *A Breath of Life*. Translated by Johnny Lorenz. New York: New Directions, 2012.

- "THE LAST WORD WILL BE THE FOURTH DIMENSION.
  Length: her speaking
  Width: beyond thought
  Depth: my speaking of her, of facts and feelings and of her beyond-thought.
  I must be legible almost in the dark"

p. 9: Bachelard, Gaston. *The Poetics of Space*. Translated by Maria Jolas. Boston: Beacon Press, 1969.

- "the house protects the dreamer"

p. 13: Jelinek, Elfriede. *Women as Lovers*. Translated by Martin Chalmers. London: Serpent's Tail, 1994.

- "to regard her body and what happens to it, as something that happens to someone else"
- "a second body"

p. 28: Kim, Eunsong. *Copy Paper: Ream 1*. Hadley, MA: Flying Object, 2015.

- "Without being caught, without disappearing"

p. 28: Beckett, Samuel. "The End." In *The Complete Short Prose 1929–1989*. Edited by S. E. Gontarski, 78–99. New York: Grove Press, 1995.

- "The scene was the familiar one of grandeur and desolation"

p. 33: Notley, Alice. "Lady Poverty." In *Mysteries of Small Houses*, 138–139. New York: Penguin Books, 1998.

- "and that starting so / poorly, I can live"

pp. 38, 41: Kane, Sarah. *4.48 Psychosis*. London: Methuen Drama, 2000.

- "Have you made any plans?"
- "After 4.48 I shall not speak again"

p. 46: Bataille, Georges. *Inner Experience*. Translated by Leslie Anne Boldt. Albany, NY: State University of New York Press, 1988.

- "method of being better than a cloth in tatters"

p. 48: Heaney, Seamus. "The Rain Stick." In *The Spirit Level.* London: Faber & Faber, 1996.

- "Listen now again"

p. 54: Bourgeois, Louise. "Selected Diary Notes: 1949–1987." *Grand Street*, no. 65 (Summer 1998): 29–38.

- "Do you remember how beautiful our past was? I do not know what you mean"

p. 55: *Un Chien Andalou*. Directed by Luis Buñuel. Paris: Les Grands Films Classiques, 1929.

- "Once upon a time / eight years later / around three in the morning / sixteen years before / in spring"

pp. 65, 69: Hay, Deborah. *Using the Sky: A Dance*. London: Routledge, 2016.

- "there is a hard head wind. my hair is blowing back"

p. 67: Pasolini, Pier Paolo. "Poet of Ashes." In *Pier Paolo Pasolini: Poet of Ashes*. Edited by Roberto Chiesi and Andrea Mancini, 11–61. Translated by Stephen Sartarelli. San Francisco: City Lights Publishers, 2007.

- "the rest of the time I lived in a lyric / – what else? – like all lunatics"

p. 69: Zambreno, Kate. *Appendix Project: Talks and Essays*. South Pasadena, CA: Semiotext(e), 2019.

- "That my body is a space where the text was still being written"

p. 70: Gordon, Avery. *Ghostly Matters: Haunting and the Sociological Imagination*. Minneapolis: University of Minnesota Press, 2008.

- "I look for her shape and his hand . . . finding the shape described by her absence"

p. 72: Manning, Erin. *Relationscapes: Movement, Art, Philosophy*. Cambridge, MA: MIT Press, 2012.

- "folds have a tendency to refold, to pleat, to crease, to wrinkle"

pp. 78, 82: Rainer, Yvonne. "From a memoir-in-progress." *Women & Performance: A Journal of Feminist Theory* 14, no. 2 (2005): 9–11.

- "It requires phenomenal control to do it slowly without faltering and wavering"
- "I had complete control"

p. 78: De Keersmaeker, Anne Teresa, and Rosas. *Fase, Four Movements to the Music of Steve Reich*. Royal Opera House, London, March 16–17, 2022.

- "Silver silk bias cut dress. White plimsolls, bottoms unmarked."

p. 79: Valéry, Paul. *Dance and the Soul.* Translated by Dorothy Bussy. London: John Lehmann, 1951.

- "She is beginning, do you see, with a walk which is wholly divine—a simple walk round"

p. 80: "Saint Laurent - Women's Summer 2022 Show," Anthony Vaccarello, 2021. https://www.youtube.com/watch?v=UfQaAhD6Vzg.

- "this girl from nowhere and she's also an illusion"

p. 81: Brown, Carol. "Inscribing the Body: Feminist Choreographic Practices." PhD diss., University of Surrey, 1994.

- "To fix in space-time and then to undo by decodings, spasms, wrenchings, blurrings and breakages. With reckless impetuous gestures - break line - break gender - break sound - break centre"

p. 81: Robertson, Lisa. *The Baudelaire Fractal.* Toronto: Coach House Books, 2020.

- "With an obscure hesitation one steps into the day and its frame and its costume"

p. 82: Sang, Yi. *The Wings*. Translated by Chŏng-hyo An and James B. Lee. Seoul: Jimoondang Publishing Company, 2001.

- "It is worth trying to counterfeit yourself"

p. 84: *Opening Night*. Directed by John Cassavetes. Faces Distribution, 1977.

- "I am not me"
- "There's someone posing here as us"

p. 84: Howe, Fanny. *London-Rose: Beauty Will Save the World*. Brussels: Divided Publishing, 2022.

- "Is it possible to be noticed by others and free?"

p. 84: Cheng, Anne Anlin. *Ornamentalism*. New York: Oxford University Press, 2019.

- "and ceramics alongside which she sits"

p. 87: Moncrieff, William Thomas. *Giselle; or, The Phantom Night Dancers.* London: J. Limbird, 1842.

- "That is the strain I loved ;—the waltz I danced to ;—the fatal Wili waltz ;—once more I'll tread its steps . . . rob me not of this last poor pleasure . . . Ah! my steps faulter—my limbs grow faint—I choke—I—"

p. 89: Artaud, Antonin. "The Nerve Meter." In *Selected Writings*. Edited by Susan Sontag, 79–87. Translated by Helen Weaver. New York: Farrar, Straus and Giroux, 1976.

- "I have only one occupation left: to remake myself"

p. 91: H. D. "Eurydice." In *Collected Poems 1912–1944*. Edited by Louis L. Martz, 51–55. New York: New Directions, 1983.

- "before I am lost, / hell must open like a red rose / for the dead to pass"

p. 93: Cha, Theresa Hak Kyung. *Dictée*. New York: Tanam Press, 1982.

- "Between the two white columns"
- "Abrasive and worn"

p. 102: *A Matter of Life and Death*. Directed by Michael Powell and Emeric Pressburger. Los Angeles, CA: Eagle-Lion Films, 1946.

- "prop or wings"

p. 105: Berssenbrugge, Mei-mei. "Permanent Home." In *I Love Artists: New and Selected Poems*, 98–101. Berkeley, CA: University of California Press, 2006.

- "while my house continues to rotate on earth"

p. 109–110: Jarman, Derek. *Up in the Air: Collected Film Scripts*. London: Vintage, 1996.

- "The Rolls Royce drives through the dereliction, sinister and silent, following its angel"

p. 113: Barthes, Roland. *The Preparation of the Novel.* Translated by Kate Briggs. New York: Columbia University Press, 2011.

- "the future of the Book is the Album, just as the ruin is the future of the monument"

ACKNOWLEDGMENTS

Texts comprising *Repose* were written between 2019 and 2022 and revised intermittently between 2022 and 2024. I am grateful for having the time and space needed to work on this book. The room I write, the room I sleep, the room I live.

Images on pages 62, 63, and 111 courtesy of the author.

Several texts were informed by a period of practice-research at Trinity Laban Conservatoire of Music & Dance and Independent Dance in London in 2019–2020, an enriching time for which I am grateful.

Variations of several texts appeared under different titles in *Datableed, Fence*, *LUMIN Journal*, *Rabbit*, and Puncher & Wattmann's *Slow Loris* pamphlet series. Thank you to the editors of these publications.

Thank you to Dzifa Benson, who read and provided feedback on drafts of the manuscript.

Thank you to the team at Wendy's Subway: Corinne Butta, for stewarding the publication process from beginning to end and for your generous editing of the manuscript, and Juwon Jun, for proofreading the work.

Thank you to Dorothy Lin, for bringing the design of the book to life.

Thank you to Asiya Wadud, guest judge of the 2022 Wendy's Subway Open Reading Period, to whom the publication of this book is owed.

To my family, for everything, as ever,

Passage Series #6
First Edition, 2024
Edition of 1,000 copies
ISBN: 979-8-9909878-0-7
Library of Congress Control Number: 2024942066

Edited by Corinne Butta
Proofread by Juwon Jun
Designed by Dorothy Lin
Typeset in Martina Plantijn and Courier
Printed at Tallinna, Estonia

Published by Wendy's Subway
379 Bushwick Avenue
Brooklyn, NY 11206
wendyssubway.com

Wendy's Subway is a non-profit reading room, writing space, and independent publisher located in Brooklyn.

The Passage Series features titles by emerging writers and artists whose work manifests in innovative, hybrid, and cross-genre forms that imagine new possibilities and expressions of the poetic, the political, and the social.

Repose is the 2022 Open Reading Period Book Prize awardee, selected by guest judge Asiya Wadud.

The Passage Series is supported, in part, by the New York State Council on the Arts with support of the Office of the Governor and the New York State Legislature; public funds from the New York City Department of Cultural Affairs in Partnership with the City Council; and the Robert Rauschenberg Foundation.